FASCINATING SCIENCE PROJECTS

AIR

Sally Hewitt

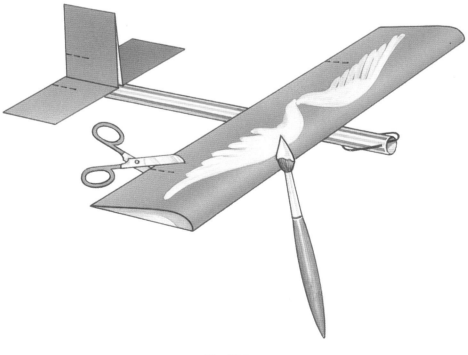

Franklin Watts
London • Sydney

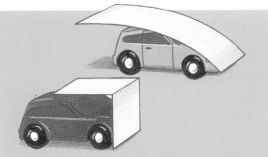

© Aladdin Books Ltd 2003
Produced by
Aladdin Books Ltd
28 Percy Street
London W1T 2BZ

ISBN 0–7496–4954–2

First published in Great Britain in 2003 by
Franklin Watts
96 Leonard Street
London
EC2A 4XD

Designers:
Flick, Book Design and Graphics
Pete Bennett

Editor:
Harriet Brown

Illustrators:
Ian Thompson,
Catherine Ward and Peter Wilks – SGA
Cartoons: Tony Kenyon – BL Kearley

Consultant:
Dr Bryson Gore

Printed in UAE

A CIP catalogue record for this book is available
from the British Library.

Contents

Introduction

In this book, the science of air is explained through a series of fascinating projects and experiments. Each chapter deals with a different topic on air, such as air pressure or air power, and contains a major project that is fully supported by simple experiments, 'Magic' panels and 'Fascinating fact' boxes. At the end of every chapter is an explanation of what has happened and the science behind it. Projects requiring the use of sharp tools, heat or chemicals should be done with adult supervision.

This states the purpose of the project

METHOD NOTES
Helpful hints on things to remember when carrying out your project.

Materials
In this box is a full list of the items needed to carry out each of the main projects.

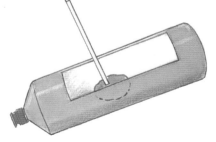

Figure 2

1. The steps that describe how to carry out each project are listed clearly as numbered points.

2. Where there are illustrations to help you understand the instructions, the text refers to them as Figure 1, etc.

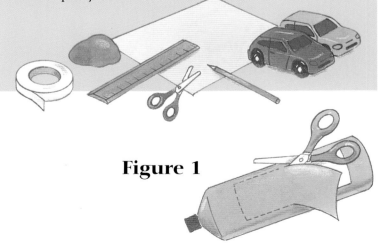

Figure 1

THE AMAZING MAGIC PANEL
This heading states what is happening

These boxes contain an activity or experiment that has a particularly dramatic or surprising result!

WHY IT WORKS
You can find out exactly what happened here.

WHAT THIS SHOWS

These boxes, which are headed either 'What this shows' or 'Why it works', contain an explanation of what should happen during your project, why it happened and the meaning of the result.

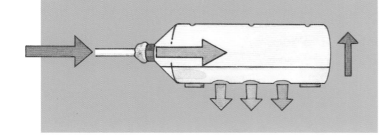

Fascinating facts!
An amusing or surprising fact related to the theme of the chapter.

Where the project involves using a sharp knife or anything else that requires adult supervision, you will see this warning symbol.

The text in these circles links the theme of the topic in each chapter from one page to the next.

What is air?

Air is a mixture of gases, mostly nitrogen, oxygen, argon and carbon dioxide, that surrounds our planet Earth. Air makes it possible for living things to survive, and Earth is the only planet we know of that is teeming with life. We can't see air, but we can feel it when we breathe it into our lungs and we can feel it pushing against us when it moves. Air is always moving, rushing into empty spaces created when other things move away.

Discover that 'empty' spaces are full of air

METHOD NOTES
A funnel with a narrow stem works best for this experiment.

Materials
- a funnel
- modelling clay
- a plastic bottle
- scissors
- a jug of water

1. Press a strip of modelling clay around the stem of the funnel (Figure 1).

2. Carefully press closed scissors into the bottle just below the bottle opening (Figure 2). Make a hole about the size of your little fingernail.

Figure 1

Figure 2

3. Roll a piece of clay into a ball to make a plug. Plug the hole you made with the clay (Figure 3).

4. Push the funnel into the empty bottle (Figure 3). Use the clay to make a seal around the funnel to stop air from escaping.

Figure 3

5. Quickly pour water through the funnel into the bottle (Figure 4). Only a trickle of water will get through at first, then the flow will stop.

6. Now pull the plug of clay out of the small hole (Figure 5). Watch the water flow freely into the bottle.

Figure 4

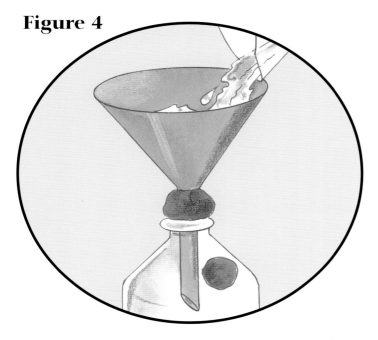

WHAT THIS SHOWS

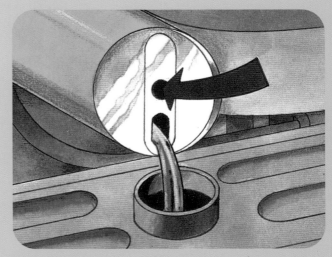

The bottle was full of air so there was no room for the water to get in. When air escapes through the small hole, the water pours into the bottle to replace the air. Oil does not pour well out of a can with only one small hole. The thick oil would block the hole as it poured out and no air could get into the can to replace the oil. So oil cans have a second hole to let air in.

Figure 5

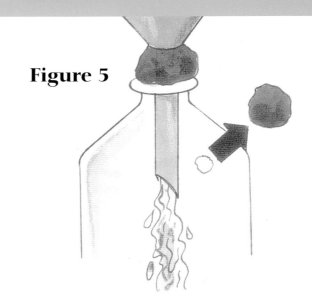

7

Animals take in oxygen from the air when they breathe. Plants take in carbon dioxide. Fumes from traffic pollute the air making it dirty and unhealthy for plants and animals.

What is air?

POLLUTION

You need two pieces of clean white cloth. Cut out two shapes from a darker coloured cloth (Figure 1). Lightly glue one shape onto each white cloth (Figure 2). Hang one cloth near a busy road and the other in a park or garden.

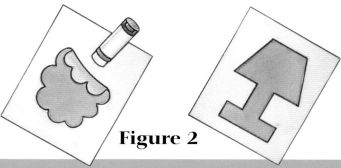

Figure 1

Collect the cloths after a couple of weeks – is one dirtier than the other? Pull off the shapes and you'll see how dirty the cloth exposed to the air has really become (Figure 3).

Figure 2

Figure 3

WHAT THIS SHOWS

The air around you doesn't usually look dirty but it can be full of tiny particles of dirt called pollution. This is what has made the cloths dirty. Rain falling through polluted air can become acid and damage trees and buildings. Exhaust fumes and factory smoke can cause thick, dirty fog called smog.

AIR EVERYWHERE

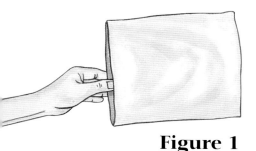

Flatten a small bag to check it's empty. Hold the edge (Figure 1) and whirl it around you. See how the air puffs it out (Figure 2).

Figure 1

Figure 2

BURNING AND AIR

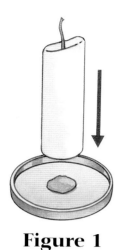

Fire needs oxygen, one of the gases in air, to burn. Fix a candle firmly on a small lid with modelling clay (Figure 1). Put it on a flat surface. Carefully light the candle (Figure 2).

Figure 1

Place a big glass jar over the candle (Figure 3). The candle will burn for a short while. When it has used most of the oxygen in the air in the jar, it will go out. Fire extinguishers work by covering flames to block out air.

Figure 2

Figure 3

No air in space!
There is no air at all in space, just emptiness between the planets, stars and galaxies. Astronauts have to take their own air with them so that they can breathe and stay alive in space.

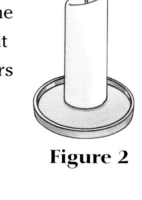

Air
is an invisible mixture of gases. It surrounds the Earth in layers – the atmosphere. On Earth, air fills all 'empty' spaces. If air can't get out of a container, you will not be able to pour anything into it.

Atmosphere

The atmosphere is the layer of air about 700 kilometres deep that surrounds the planet Earth. It keeps us warm and protects us from the Sun's harmful rays. The atmosphere doesn't float off into space because a force called gravity pulls it towards Earth and holds it in place. Air becomes thinner and colder the further away it is from the Earth's surface. The layer nearest the Earth is called the troposphere. This is where the weather takes place.

Make a barometer to forecast the weather

METHOD NOTES
Use a large balloon with strong rubber that won't split when you stretch it.

Materials
- a balloon
- scissors
- a glass jar
- an elastic band
- sticky tape
- a toothpick
- a drinking straw
- card
- coloured pens

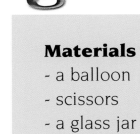

1. Cut off the neck and about a quarter of the balloon with the scissors (Figure 1).

2. Stretch the balloon as tightly as you can without splitting the rubber, and pull it over the opening of the jar (Figure 2). Hold it in place with an elastic band.

Figure 1

Figure 2

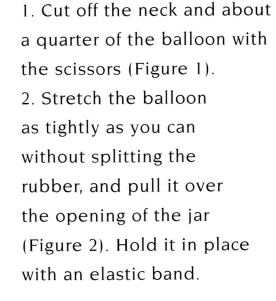

10

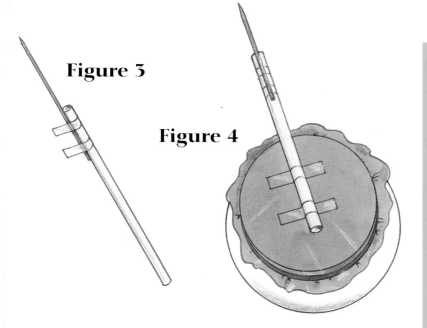

Figure 3

Figure 4

3. Tape the toothpick to one end of the straw (Figure 3).

4. Tape the other end of the straw to the balloon on the jar (Figure 4).

5. Cut a strip of card about 10 cm taller than the jar. Fold back 5 cm of it to make a stand (Figure 5).

6. Draw a sun for sunny weather at

Figure 5

the top of the card and a cloud for rain about halfway down (Figure 5).

7. Place your barometer with the toothpick pointing between the sun and the cloud (Figure 6).

8. Look at it every day and mark a line where the toothpick is pointing between the symbols.

WHAT THIS SHOWS

Air is pushed down by the weight of the air above it – called atmospheric pressure (see pages 18-21). (a) High pressure pushes down on the balloon making the pointer move up.

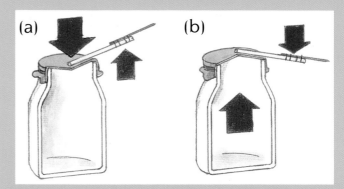

This means the weather will be sunny. (b) Low pressure causes air in the jar to rise, pushing the balloon up. The pointer moves down to show cloudy weather.

Figure 6

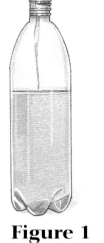

The air found in the troposphere contains lots of water. We can't usually see the water. This is because the water is often in the form of an invisible gas called water vapour.

Atmosphere

MAKE CLOUDS IN A BOTTLE

Carefully fill a clear plastic bottle with hot water (Figure 1). Leave it for a few seconds (Figure 2) then pour half the water away (Figure 3).

Quickly put an ice cube in the bottle opening (Figure 4). Water vapour rises up from the hot water and cools down when it gets near the ice cube. As it cools, the water vapour turns into liquid in the form of tiny water droplets. They steam up the top of the bottle and make a cloud.

Figure 1

Figure 2

Figure 3

Figure 4

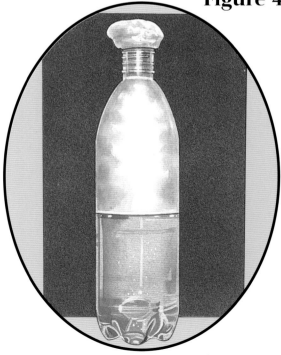

WHAT THIS SHOWS

Hot air rises, so when the ground is warmed by the Sun, air near the ground is also warmed. This warm air rises. Air gets cooler the further away from the ground it gets. As in your experiment, as the rising air cools, the water vapour changes into water droplets so tiny that they stay in the air and form a cloud.

THE AMAZING INVISIBLE DRAWING
See how water vapour in the air can reveal a picture

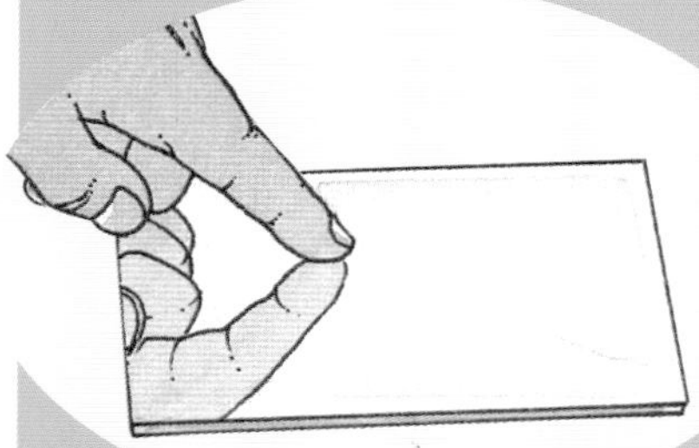

Put a mirror in the fridge for a few minutes. Draw a face on it with your finger. Water vapour in the air turns into droplets on the cold mirror. Heat the mirror with a hair dryer to see the face disappear.

WHY IT WORKS
Water droplets won't form where you drew the face because of natural oil from your skin. When you blow warm air on the mirror, water droplets evaporate. Put the mirror back into the fridge. Does the face return?

MAKE A WIND DETECTOR

Wind is moving air. It moves when warm air rises and colder air moves in to fill the space it has left. Cut out rectangles of tissue paper, writing paper, tin foil, and thin and thick card (Figure 1).

Make a hole in each paper and attach a length of string (Figure 2). Tie the papers along a stick with the lightest at the top and the heaviest at the bottom. Fix the wind detector outside. A light breeze will just move the tissue paper. A strong wind will move all five papers.

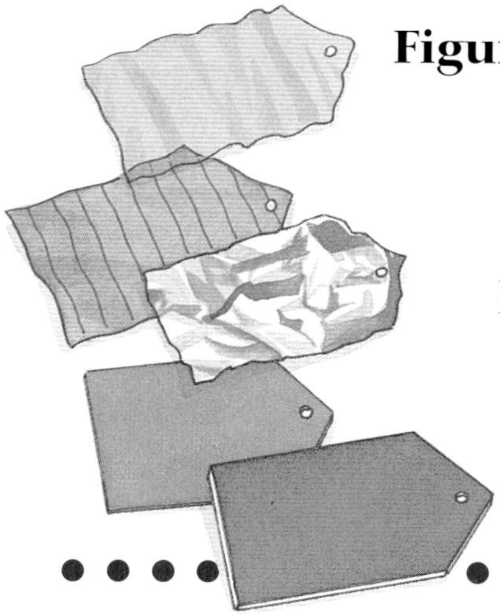

Figure 1

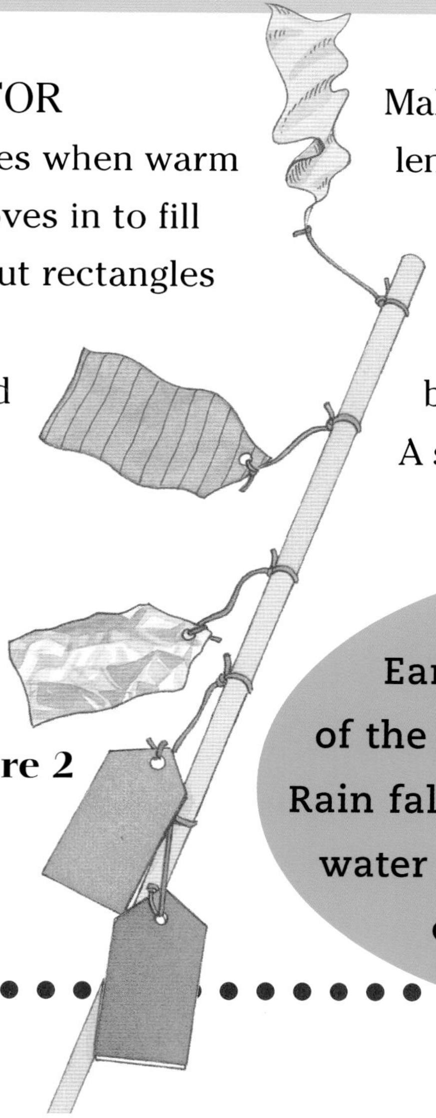

Figure 2

Planet
Earth has weather because of the atmosphere surrounding it. Rain falls because of tiny droplets of water in the atmosphere. Wind is caused by moving air.

Weight of air

Like everything around you, air has weight caused by gravity pulling it towards the centre of the Earth. Density is the weight of something compared to its size. Air is less dense than water – one gram of air takes up more space than one gram of water. Air is a gas and doesn't have a shape, so it is difficult to weigh. But air will flow and fill an empty container. You can compare the weight of a container filled with air and one the same size filled with water.

See how air helps your submarine to float

METHOD NOTES
You can buy plastic tubing from a hardware store.

Figure 1

Materials
- pointed scissors
- a plastic squeezy bottle
- waterproof sticky tape
- a length of plastic tube
- modelling clay
- a bowl of water
- two coins

1. Cut three holes about the size of your fingernail along one side of the bottle (Figure 1).
2. Tape a coin on either side of the holes to add weight to the bottle (Figure 1).

3. Use the scissors to pierce the other side of the bottle with three little holes.
4. Push the end of the tubing into the small opening of the lid (Figure 2).
5. Seal the tubing in the hole with modelling clay (Figure 3).

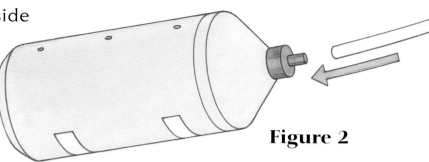

Figure 2

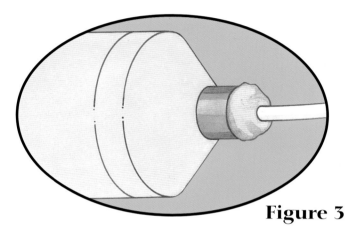

Figure 3

6. Put the submarine in the bowl and let it fill with water and sink.
7. Blow into the tube to fill the submarine with air and make it rise (Figure 4). Let the air out through the tube to make the submarine sink again.

Figure 4

WHY IT WORKS

Air is less dense than water so the submarine is lighter when it is filled with air than when it is filled with water. Blowing through the tube forces water out and lets air flow in. When the submarine is filled with air, it rises to the surface.

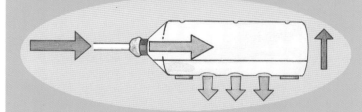

When you stop blowing, air flows out of the submarine through the little holes and the tube. It fills with water and sinks. Real submarines have tanks that are filled with water to make them sink. When a submarine wants to return to the surface, the water is replaced by air and it rises.

15

Weight of air

When we say things are empty, they are probably full of air. A space with nothing in it at all, not even air, is called a vacuum. There is no air in outer space.

WEIGH AIR

Tie string around the middle of a long, thin stick. Tape blown-up balloons to either end – the balloons must be the same size.

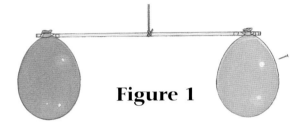

Figure 1

Figure 2

Hold the string and the balloons should balance. Now burst one of the balloons (Figure 1). The balloon with air in it will make the balance tip down showing that letting air out of the other balloon has made it lighter (Figure 2).

As heavy as an elephant?!
Air is much heavier than you would imagine. Air presses down on 1 square metre of the ground with the same weight as a large elephant.

THE AMAZING DRY TISSUE
See how a tissue in a glass stays dry when plunged into water

Crumple a tissue and wedge it into the bottom of a glass. Upturn the glass and plunge it into a bowl of water. Take the glass out of the water and pull out the tissue – it is quite dry!

WHY IT WORKS
The glass is full of air so water can't get in. Air is lighter than water so it can't push water out of the way and get out of the glass – so the tissue stays dry.

PEN LID DIVER

Choose a pen lid without a hole in the top. Fix enough modelling clay onto the pen lid so that it floats as in Figure 1. Stretch a piece of balloon over the jar opening and fix it with an elastic band. Press on the rubber and watch the lid dive (Figure 2). Release and watch the lid rise.

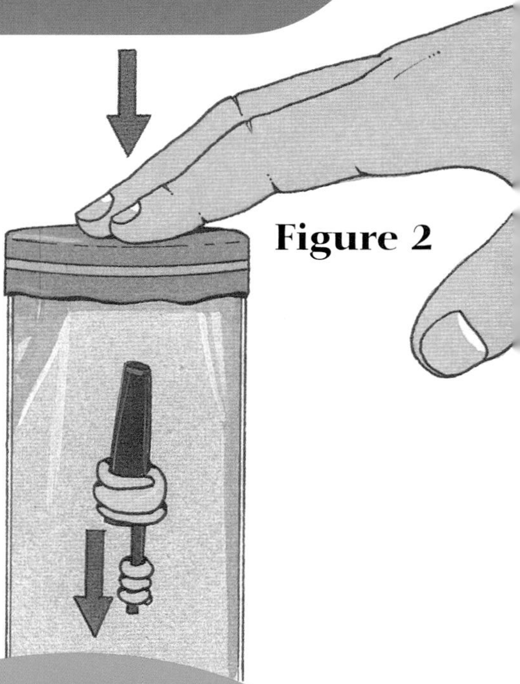

Figure 1

Figure 2

WHY IT WORKS
A bubble of air in the tip of the lid makes it float. Pressing on the rubber squeezes the air in the pen lid. There is then extra room for water inside the lid. The lid gets heavier and sinks.

Air has weight, but we say "as light as air" because air is light for its size compared with other substances, such as water.

Air pressure

Air pressure is caused by the weight of air being pulled down on the Earth's surface. Air presses from all directions – on every side and from underneath as well as from above. Air pressure is at its greatest near the ground. The further away from the ground, the lower air pressure becomes. Air pressure is so low thousands of metres above the ground that you wouldn't be able to breathe. So aeroplanes have pressurised air in the cabin so that people on board can breathe normally.

See air pressure make a card hover

METHOD NOTES
Use a cotton reel that is solid apart from the hole in the middle.

Materials
- scissors
- card
- a drawing pin
- a drinking straw
- a cotton reel

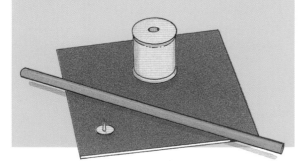

Figure 1

1. Cut a square of card about 12 x 12 cm. Mark the centre point of the card and push a drawing pin through it (Figure 1).
2. Push the straw through the hole in one end of the cotton reel. Place the other end over the sharp point of the drawing pin (Figure 2).

Figure 2

3. Lift up the card, keeping the point of the drawing pin in the bottom hole of the cotton reel. This helps to keep the card in place.

4. Blow down the straw so that a stream of air goes down the hole in the cotton reel onto the card (Figure 3).

5. Let go of the card. It should hover in the air just below the cotton reel. Experiment with the size of the card to see what works best.

Figure 3

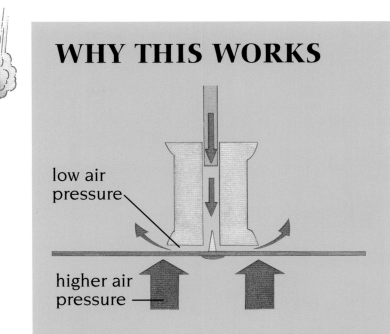

WHY THIS WORKS

low air pressure

higher air pressure

As you blow air through the gap between the cotton reel and the card, you create an area of low pressure. Air pressure pushing up on the card from underneath has more power than the moving air pushing it down. These two forces make the card hover.

Hovering football pitch

The Sapporo Dome in Japan has an indoor and an outdoor football stadium. The football pitch hovers on a cushion of high pressure air. It can be floated indoors when it rains. The higher air pressure under the pitch holds it up.

When cold air sinks, it creates an area of high pressure. When hot air rises it creates an area of low pressure. Cold air moves in to take the place of hot air.

Air pressure

UPSIDEDOWN GLASS OF WATER

You can turn a glass of water upside down without spilling a drop with the help of air pressure. Do this over a sink the first time! First, fill a glass to the brim with water (Figure 1). Slide a piece of stiff card over the top of the glass and hold it in place (Figure 2).

Figure 1

Figure 2

Figure 3

Now, still holding the card in place, quickly turn the glass upside down (Figure 3). Then, hold the glass with one hand and let go of the card. The water magically stays in the glass (Figure 4).

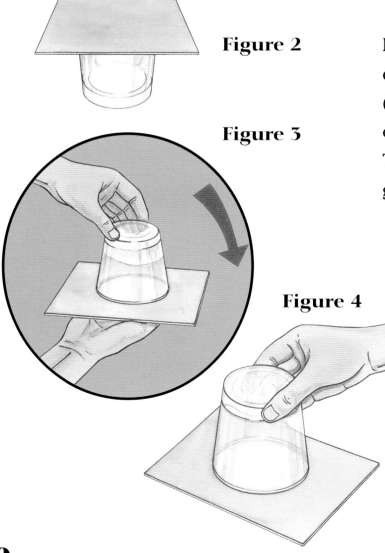

Figure 4

WHAT THIS SHOWS

Air pressure pushing up on the card is stronger than the force of the water pushing down on it. So, the strong air pressure outside the glass holds the card in place. This stops the water from falling out of the glass.

THE AMAZING EGG
See air pressure squeeze an egg

1. Ask an adult to help you hard boil an egg for about 10 minutes. Then use a spoon to drop it in cold water.
2. Take off the shell.
3. Balance it, pointed end down, in the opening of a glass carafe or vase with a narrow neck to check it won't fall through.
4. Take out the egg. Put a crumpled kitchen towel into the vase and ask an adult to light it.
5. Quickly put back the egg and watch it shrink and fall into the bottle.

WHY IT WORKS
The fire heats up, and expands the air in the vase. When the fire goes out, the air cools down and contracts. The air pressure in the vase gets lower. The egg forms a seal at the opening of the vase. The air pressure outside is higher than in the vase. So the egg is pushed into the vase.

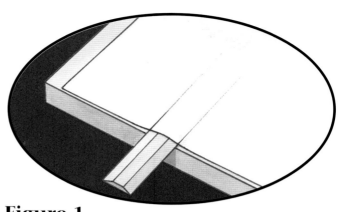

Figure 1

STRONG AIR PRESSURE
Lie a ruler with its end just over the edge of a table. Put a sheet of paper over the ruler (Figure 1) and sharply tap the end of the ruler (Figure 2). Feel how difficult it is to lift the paper. You can feel air pressure pressing down on the paper.

Figure 2

Air pressure is created by the weight of air pressing down on Earth. Even though it presses on us from all sides, you can't usually feel it.

Compressed air

Air, like everything in the universe, is made up of atoms and molecules. Atoms are the smallest particles that anything can be divided into. Molecules are made up of two or more atoms. Air is a mixture of gases. Gas molecules are much more spread out than the molecules that make up solids and liquids. The spaces between air molecules are big enough to allow air to be squashed into a smaller space and create what is called compressed air.

Launch a rocket with compressed air

METHOD NOTES
You can roll a cylinder of card and use it instead of the wider drinking straw.

Materials
- a wide drinking straw
- card and scissors
- modelling clay and sticky tape
- a narrow drinking straw
- a squeezy bottle

Figure 1

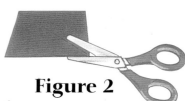

Figure 2

Figure 3

1. Cut off 4 cm from the end of the wide straw. Mould a rocket nose with the modelling clay and put it on one end (Figure 1).
2. Cut out two card triangles (Figure 2). Stick them on the other end of the wide straw with sticky tape (Figure 3).

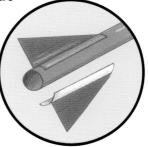

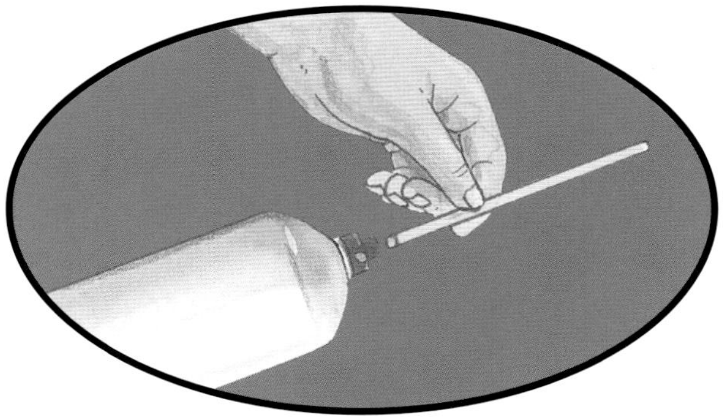

Figure 4

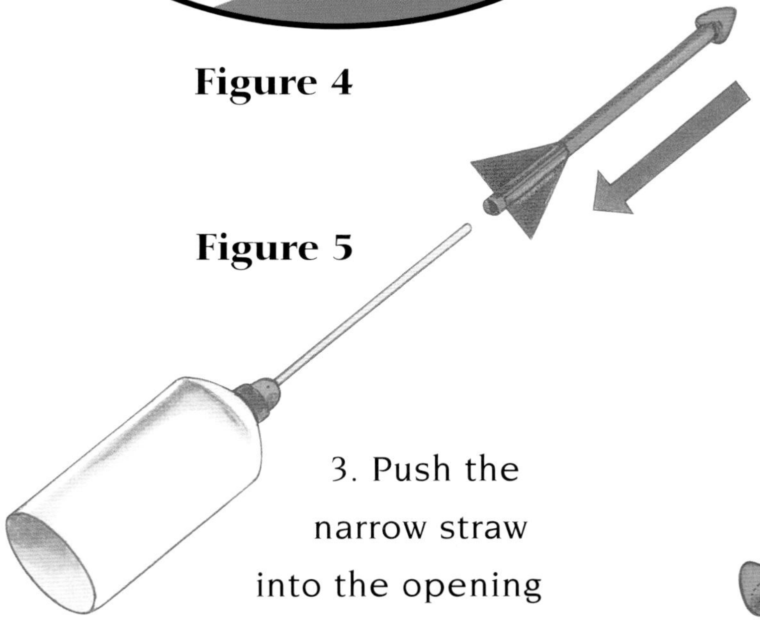

Figure 5

3. Push the
narrow straw
into the opening
of the squeezy bottle
nozzle (Figure 4) and fix it with
modelling clay to make it airtight.
4. Squeeze the bottle with one
hand and feel air puffing through
the end of the straw with your other
hand to make sure air is flowing through.
5. Put the large straw, which is now your
rocket, over the narrow straw, which is your
launcher (Figure 5).
6. Squeeze the bottle firmly to launch your rocket
with a puff of air (Figure 6). Make sure you don't
fire it directly at anyone.

WHY IT WORKS

When you squeeze the bottle, you
are making the space inside the
bottle smaller. If the bottle lid was
firmly shut, air inside the bottle
would be squashed
or compressed into
the smaller space.
In your launcher, the
compressed air
escapes through the
narrow straw with
enough force to
push the rocket
into the air.

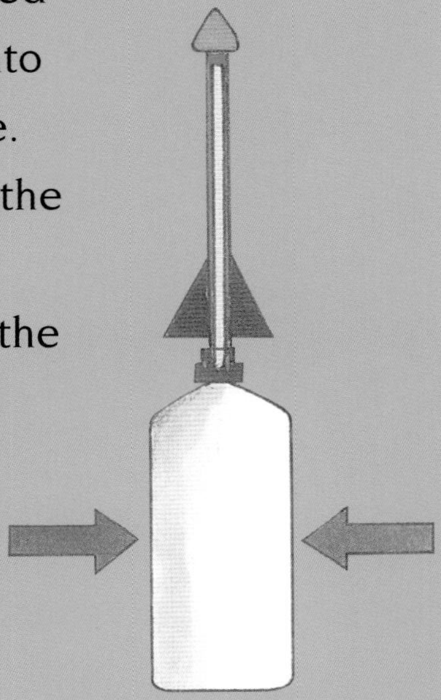

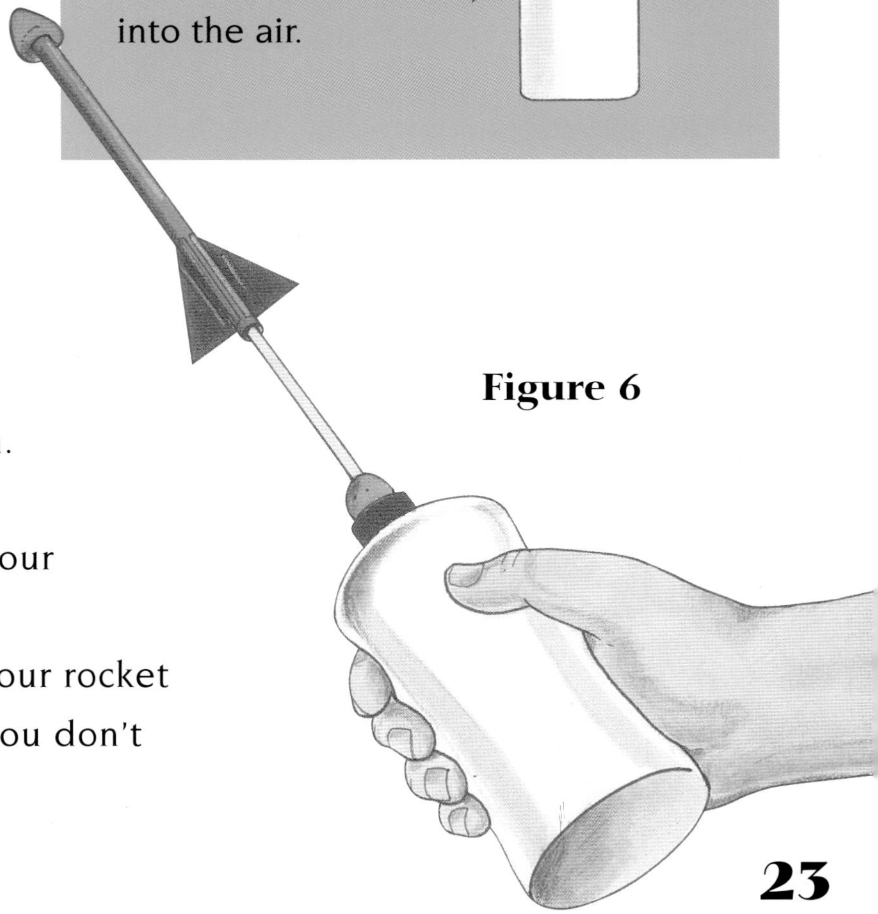

Figure 6

Compressed air

MAKE A HELICOPTER

Cut a square of card 10 x 10 cm. Copy the pattern shown (Figure 1) onto the card. Cut out the four shaded shapes. Fold along the other eight lines by bending one flap up and the next down, all the way around (Figure 2).

Push a thin dowelling rod or cocktail stick through the centre of the rotor. Fix it with sticky tape (Figure 3). Stand the stick in a cotton reel (Figure 4). Wind a thread around the stick and pull it quickly to spin the rotor (Figure 5) and make the helicopter rise into the air.

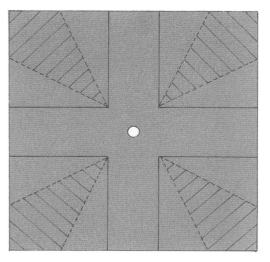

Figure 1

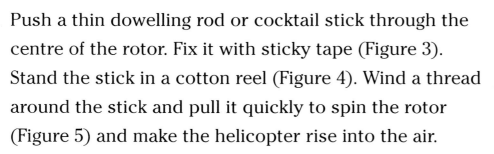

Figure 2   **Figure 3**

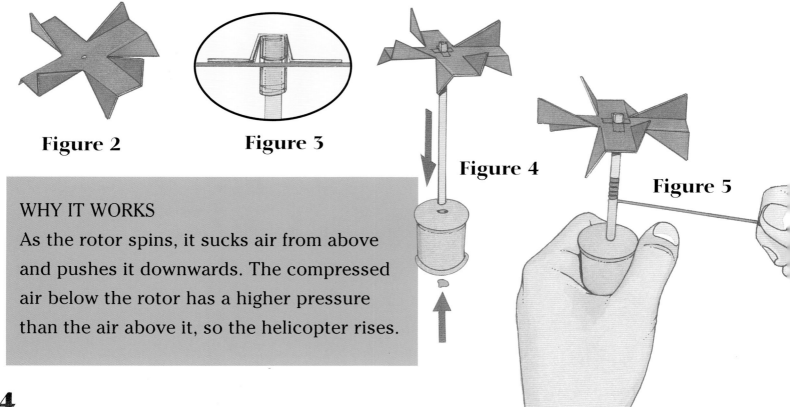

Figure 4

Figure 5

WHY IT WORKS

As the rotor spins, it sucks air from above and pushes it downwards. The compressed air below the rotor has a higher pressure than the air above it, so the helicopter rises.

THE AMAZING RISING BOOKS
See compressed air lift a pile of books

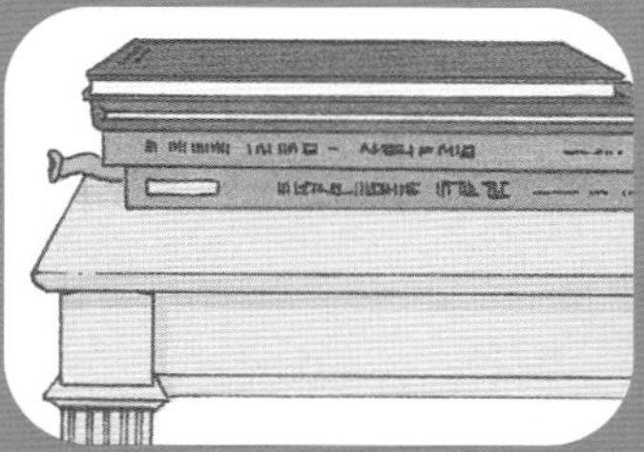

Hide a balloon under a pile of books with just the neck showing. Amaze your friends by saying you can make the books rise just using air. Blow up the balloon and they will see the books lift up!

WHY IT WORKS
As you blow, you squash more and more air into the balloon. The balloon fills with compressed air and lifts up the books.

MAKE A PUMP

Find two cardboard tubes, one just wider than the other. Tape a circle of card over one end of each tube (Figure 1). Pierce a hole in the card on the wider tube. Push the covered end of the narrow tube into the wider tube. Pump it in and out to compress the air in the wide tube and push it out of the hole (Figure 2). Try pumping air onto a balloon to push it along (Figure 3).

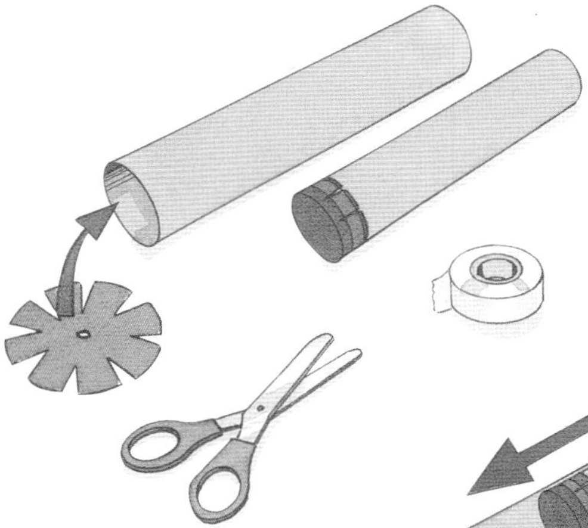

Figure 1

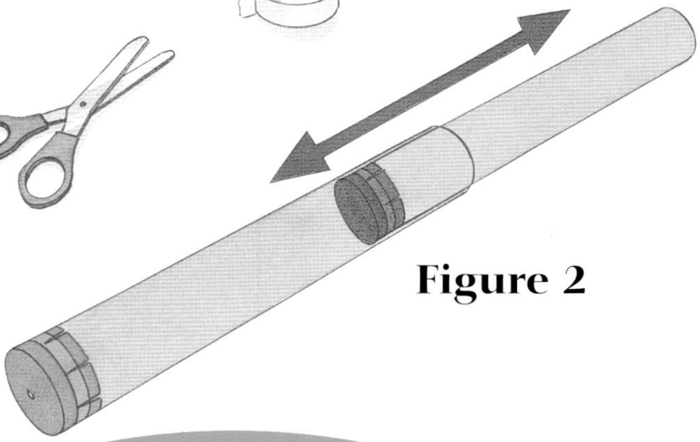

Figure 2

Figure 3

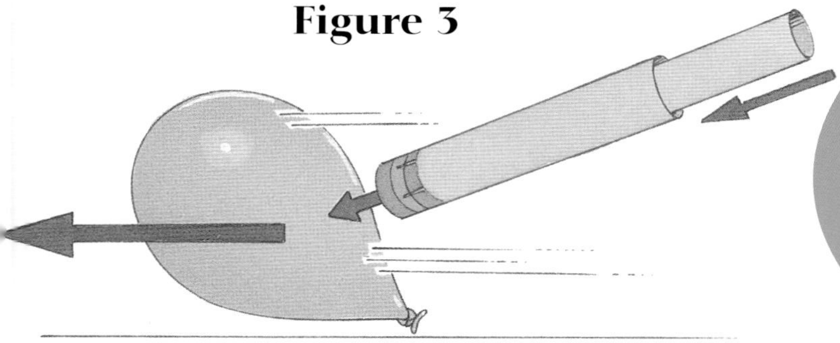

Air is a mixture of gas molecules that can move, flow and be squashed, or compressed. Compressed air fills the tyres of bikes and cars and the wheels of aeroplanes.

Hot and cold air

Air, like other things, gets bigger when it gets hotter. This is called expansion. It shrinks when it cools down. This is called contraction. Expansion happens because hot air molecules move faster and bump harder into each other than cold air molecules, causing them to take up more space. Hot air rises because it is lighter than cold air, allowing heavier cold air to sink and move in to take its place – so air is constantly on the move indoors and outside.

Make a balloon rise using hot air

METHOD NOTES
If you seal the edges of the balloon, air cannot escape and it will rise more easily.

Materials
- tissue paper
- a pencil
- a ruler
- scissors and sticky tape
- a small sheet of paper
- cotton thread
- a hairdryer
- glue

1. Draw a cross shape on tissue paper. Draw tabs along one side of each section (Figure 1). Cut it out.

2. Do the same on the sheet of paper but make this cross much smaller.

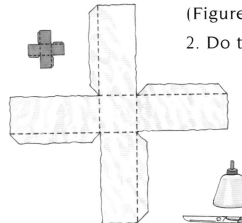

Figure 1

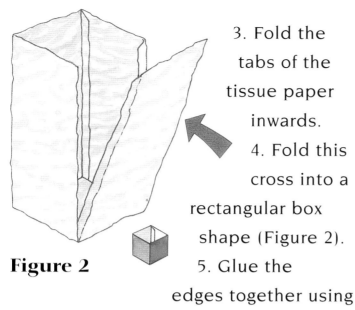

Figure 2

3. Fold the tabs of the tissue paper inwards.

4. Fold this cross into a rectangular box shape (Figure 2).

5. Glue the edges together using the tabs to make your balloon.

6. Do the same with the paper cross to make a small box (Figure 2).

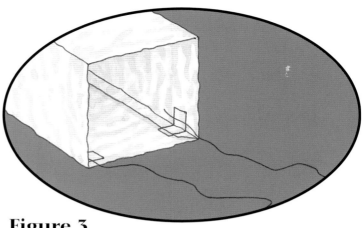

Figure 3

7. Tape four equal lengths of cotton thread into the bottom corners of the balloon (Figure 3). Tape the loose ends to the small box.

8. Take your balloon outside and blow hot air from a hairdryer into the opening of your balloon (Figure 4).

9. Watch the hot-air balloon rise up to the sky.

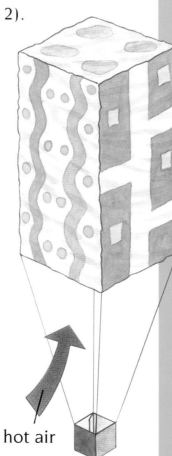

hot air

Figure 4

WHY IT WORKS

The hairdryer fills your balloon with expanding hot air and makes it rise in the colder air of the room. The balloon rises because the hot air inside it is lighter than the colder air around it. The tissue paper is a very light material, making it easier for the balloon to rise. A gas burner heats up the air inside a full-size hot-air balloon. Hot-air balloons are made from silk or very light nylon and are able to carry several people.

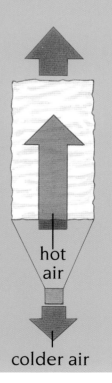

hot air

colder air

Hot and cold air

Hot air and cold air are carried around in a circular motion called a convection current. You can see shimmering air above a candle – this is the hot air rising.

BOTTLE FOUNTAIN

Make a bottle fountain and discover that as hot air expands, it becomes quite a strong force. You will need a glass bottle with a screw top. Unscrew the bottle top and carefully punch a hole in it with scissors (Figure 1). Half fill the bottle with cold water and add some food colouring. Screw the top back on, push the straw through the hole and seal it with some modelling clay (Figure 2). Put the bottle in a bowl and fill the bowl with hot water (Figure 3). Leave it for a few minutes and see the coloured water spurt out of the top of the bottle (Figure 4).

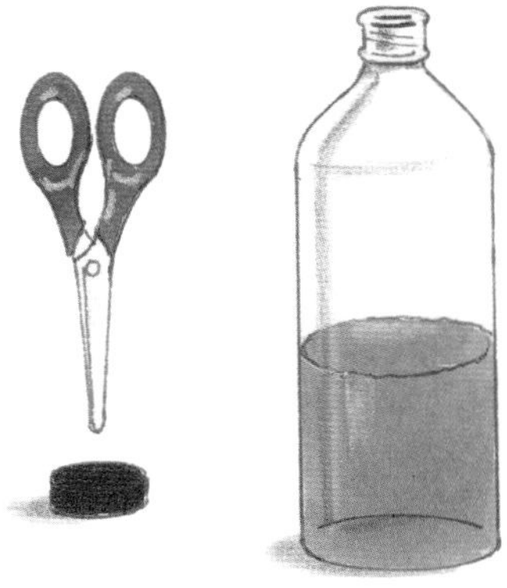

Figure 1

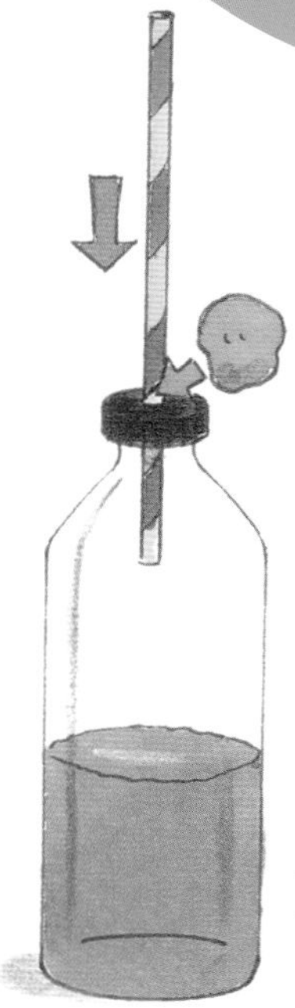

Figure 2

Figure 3

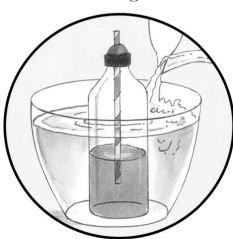

Figure 4

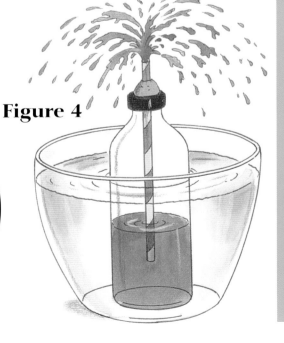

WHY IT WORKS

The hot water in the bowl heats the air in the bottle. As the air heats up, the air molecules move faster and further apart. So the air expands and pushes down on the coloured water. This forces the water up the straw and out in a spray at the top.

THE AMAZING SUCKING BOTTLE
See how cold air can suck a balloon into a bottle

Warm a glass bottle by filling it with hot water. Pour the water away. Stretch a balloon over the bottle opening and put the bottle in cold water. The balloon is sucked inside the bottle and begins to inflate.

WHY IT WORKS
The cold water makes the air in the bottle contract. Warm air rushes in to take up the extra space. It pushes the balloon in with it.

COLLAPSING BOTTLE

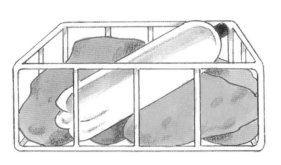

Screw the lid tightly on an empty plastic bottle (Figure 1). Put it in the freezer (Figure 2) and leave it for 10 minutes. When you take it out, the sides of the bottle will have collapsed (Figure 3). After a few minutes out of the freezer, the bottle will go back to its normal shape.

Figure 1

WHAT THIS SHOWS

The cold air contracts and takes up less space in the bottle. The lid is screwed on and no more air can get in. Instead the sides are pulled in. When the air in the bottle warms up, it expands, pushing out the sides.

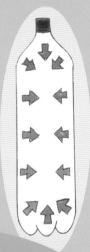

Figure 2

Figure 3

When hot air expands and cold air contracts it creates a force that pushes against things. This force can make some objects move and change shape.

Pockets of air

Nearly everything around you is full of air because air will move into spaces and fill them however big or small they are. There is air in tiny holes in your slice of bread and in the bricks your home is built with. Even water is full of air. Air trapped in layers between your clothes and in pockets in your sweater helps to stop heat escaping from your body. This is because air doesn't conduct heat very well. Using pockets and layers of air to keep things warm is called insulation.

Discover how air can keep things warm

METHOD NOTES
If you can't find a thermometer, use your finger to test the water temperature.

Materials
- 4 jars
- a cardboard box
- a newspaper
- a scarf
- a thermometer
- sticky tape

1. Put the first jar in a small cardboard box. Surround it with crumpled newspaper so that the space between the box and the jar is filled (Figure 1).

Figure 1

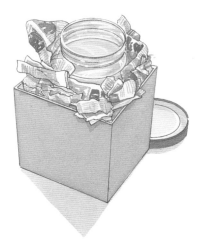

2. Wrap the second jar in a scarf or woolly jumper (Figure 2). Make sure you don't wrap it too tightly.

Figure 2

3. Tightly wrap the third jar with newspaper. Tape it in place (Figure 3).

4. Leave the fourth jar unwrapped.

5. Fill each jar with warm water and put the lids on.

6. Leave all four jars outside on a cold day or in a cold room for about half an hour.

7. Remove the lids one by one, taking the temperature of the water in each jar (Figure 4). Are the first two jars the warmest? Is the fourth jar the coldest?

Figure 3

Figure 4

WHAT THIS SHOWS

Heat escapes quickly from warm things into cold air around it. The water in the first two jars stays warm because the newspaper and the scarf trap pockets of warm air between the jars and the cold air. Trapped air does not conduct heat well and this helps to stop the heat escaping. The third jar has less trapped air around it and the fourth jar has none. Double glazing keeps a house warm by trapping air between two panes of glass. Heat cannot be easily conducted through this layer of air.

Pockets of air

Cooks use air in all kinds of recipes. They sieve flour to trap air between the grains to help their bread and cake mixtures to rise. Beating a mixture with a whisk also adds air.

MAKE MERINGUES

Separate the yolk from the white of two eggs (Figure 1). Use a whisk or an electric mixer to beat the egg whites until they are white and fluffy (Figure 2).

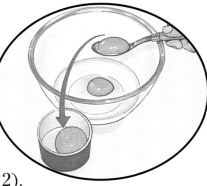

Figure 1

Mix in 175 grams of caster sugar (Figure 3) – do this gently so that the egg whites don't collapse. Spread the mixture on an oiled baking tray (Figure 4) and cook for 1 hour in the oven at 150°C. Add some fruit for a delicious dessert.

WHY IT WORKS

Whisking egg whites fills them with pockets of air. When you bake the mixture, the air pockets heat and expand to make the meringue light and fluffy. The mixture dries out in the oven to make sweet, crumbly meringue.

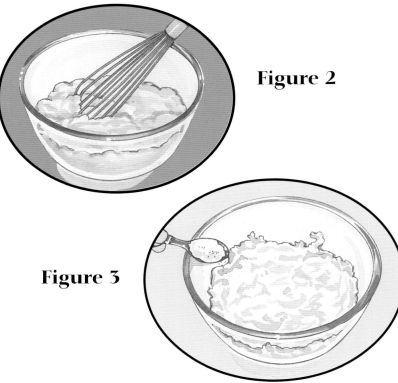

Figure 2

Figure 3

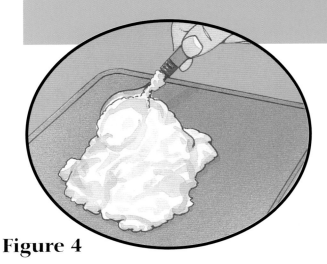

Figure 4

Figure 1

FULL OF AIR

Water is full of air – watch bubbles of air forming in a glass of warm water (Figure 1). Collect a cork, a piece of sponge, a piece of terracotta flowerpot and a teaspoon of soil. Drop each one into a glass of water. As air escapes from them, you will see bubbles of air rising up in the water (Figures 2-5).

Stick a coin to the cork to help it sink

Figure 2   **Figure 3**

Figure 4   **Figure 5**

Flying through air

Most aircraft wings are an aerofoil shape (see page 37). This gives the aircraft lift. Helicopters have spinning blades to lift them off the ground and keep them flying through the air. Aeroplanes have wings and powerful engines to fly long distances. Gliders are made of light material and have long thin wings to help them float on currents of rising warm air called thermals. Birds, bats and insects flap their wings to fly. Some birds also use thermals to glide in the same way as a glider.

Make a glider that flies through the air

METHOD NOTES
Adjust the position and shape of the wings, tail and nose to make the glider fly further.

Materials
- light card
- scissors
- a ruler
- a pencil
- sticky tape
- a drinking straw
- a paper clip
- a paintbrush
- paint

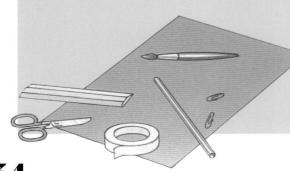

1. Cut a rectangle of card 30 x 10 cm. Draw a line lengthways so one side of the card is 6 cm wide and the other is 4 cm wide (Figure 1).

Figure 1

2. Fold along the line. Tape the two long edges together so that the wider side is curved upwards to make the wings into an aerofoil shape (Figure 2).

Figure 2

Figure 3

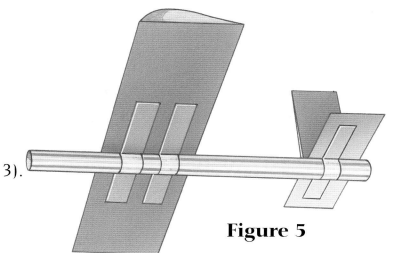

Figure 4

3. Cut a rectangle of card 6 x 2.5 cm (Figure 3). Fold it in half and in half again. Push the middle fold up (Figure 4) to make the tail.
4. Tape the straw to the middle of the underside of the wings and tail (Figure 5).
5. Attach a paper clip to the straw on the nose of the glider to add weight, and cut slits as shown by the dotted lines to make the flaps (Figure 6). The glider should balance with both wing tips resting on your fingers.
6. Paint your glider.
7. Hold the glider high, let it go and watch it glide through the air.
8. Try bending the flaps you made, to make it fly in different directions.

Figure 5

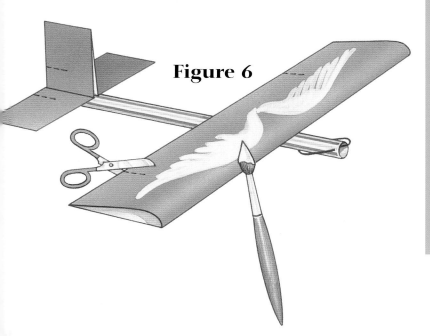

Figure 6

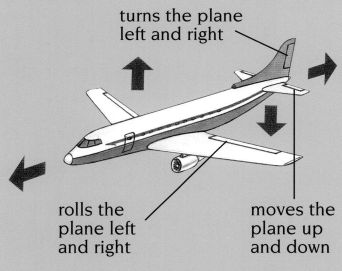

WHAT THIS SHOWS

A glider has no engine but it flies like an aeroplane.

turns the plane left and right

rolls the plane left and right

moves the plane up and down

As it moves forwards air rushes over the wings and tail fins, keeping it in the air. The flaps on the wings and tail surfaces control the direction of the aircraft.

Flying through air

Aeroplanes fly because the shape of their wings gives them lift and engines give them speed. Rocket and jet engines work by using the pushing power of hot gases.

ROCKET ENGINE

Cut out a semicircle from a large piece of card. The straight edge needs to be about 40 cm long. Fold it round, tape it and trim the edge to make a cone with a wide opening (Figure 1).

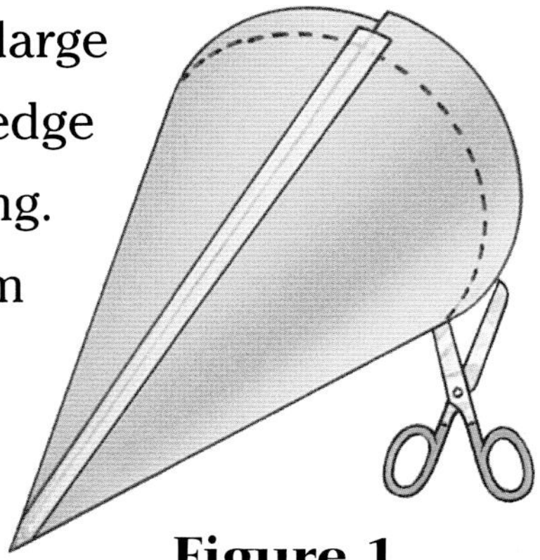

Fold a rectangle of card in half, and cut out a triangle shape with a flap along the long side, as in Figure 2. Fold the flaps back (Figure 3) and tape them to the edge of the cone (Figure 4). Repeat this until you have four triangles. Blow up a balloon and push it inside the rocket. Let go of the neck and watch the rocket take off as the air in the balloon escapes (Figure 5).

Figure 1

Figure 2

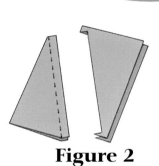

Figure 3

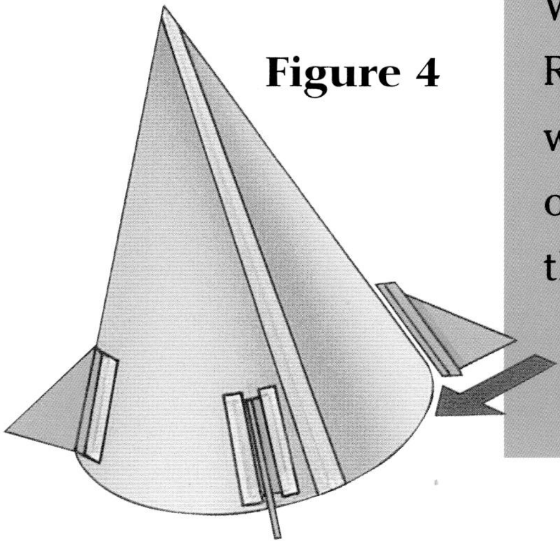

Figure 4

WHAT THIS SHOWS

Rockets take air, in liquid form, with them into space. They push out air and hot gases to move through space. Air rushing out of the balloon pushes your rocket in a similar way.

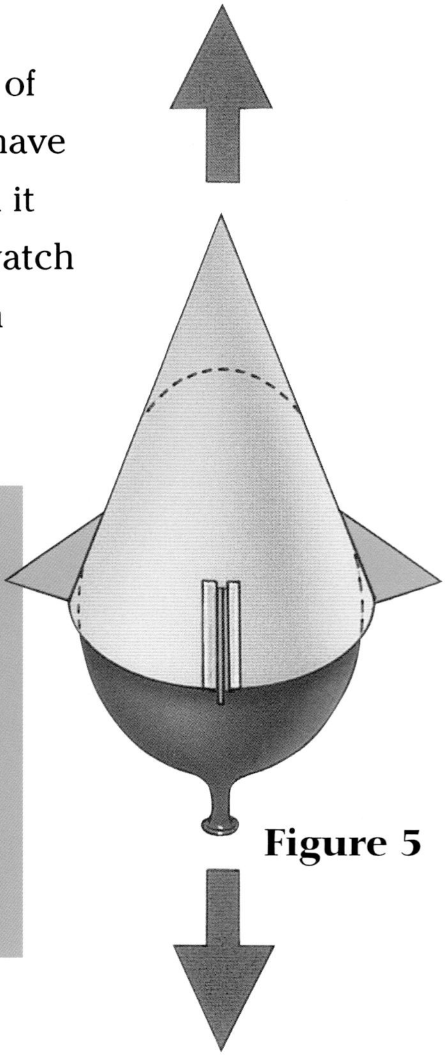

Figure 5

The incredibly short flight

Orville Wright was the first man to get an aircraft off the ground and fly it through the air. His flight didn't last long. Just 12 seconds after take-off, he crashed.

Figure 1

Figure 2

Figure 3

Direction of air

MAKE A WING

Fold over a rectangle of card and tape the edges to make a curved wing (Figure 1). Punch four holes in it with a pencil (Figure 2) and thread through two straws. Ask a friend to hold the two straws and use a hairdryer to blow air over the wing. Watch it rise (Figure 3).

WHY THIS WORKS
Air flows quickly over the wing top creating low pressure. Air flowing underneath is slower so the pressure is higher. This pushes the wing up.

Rockets
and jet engines fly in different ways. Jet engines suck in air and push it out. Rockets contain all the liquid air they need, and fly by pushing it out very fast.

Moving shapes

When you run fast you can feel air pushing against you. It ruffles your hair and clothes even when the wind isn't blowing. Sprinters, downhill skiers and cyclists wear tight, shiny clothes that don't catch the air and slow them down. Aeroplanes, boats and cars designed to go fast have pointed shapes and are made of smooth material so that air slips over them easily. These smooth, pointed shapes are called streamlined.

Discover what helps a car to move quickly

METHOD NOTES
The longer the ramp you can set up, the better this experiment will work.

Materials
- two toy cars
- card
- scissors
- a ruler
- sticky tape
- a pencil
- modelling clay
- a hairdryer and a long board

1. Find two identical cars made of light material and with wheels that turn easily.
2. Cut out two card rectangles (Figure 1). They should each be slightly wider and about 10 cm longer than the cars.

Figure 1

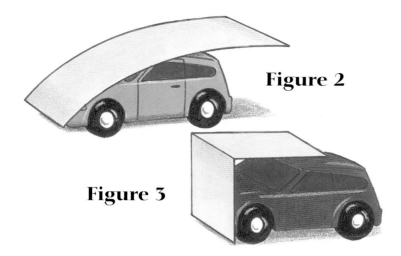

Figure 2

Figure 3

3. Tape a rectangle to the front of each car. Curve the first smoothly over the top of the car (Figure 2). Fold the second to make a right angle (Figure 3).

4. Make a ramp with a long board or book. Let the cars roll down the ramp (Figure 4) while you blow a stream of air from a hairdryer against them.

Does the car with the curved shape go faster?

Figure 4

WHAT THIS SHOWS

The car with the square shaped card is not streamlined. As it runs down the ramp, the flat front disturbs the air it is moving through. This creates a force called drag, which slows the car down.

Air slips easily over the curved card and creates less drag, which allows the car to go faster. Air rubs against a rough surface and causes friction. So smooth, shiny card helps with streamlining the vehicle.

Moving shapes

of things that move through the air can be designed either to help them go faster or to slow them down. A parachute is shaped to trap air and slow down a fall.

TRAP AIR IN AN UMBRELLA

Run along as fast as you can for a little way. Now run along holding a closed umbrella out behind you. It doesn't make much difference to your speed. Now open the umbrella and run fast holding it behind you. You can feel the umbrella slowing you down and making running feel like hard work.

WHAT THIS SHOWS

As you run, air gets caught and squashed in the open umbrella. This compressed air pushes against the umbrella and drags you backwards, slowing you down. Space shuttles use parachutes in this way to slow down when landing.

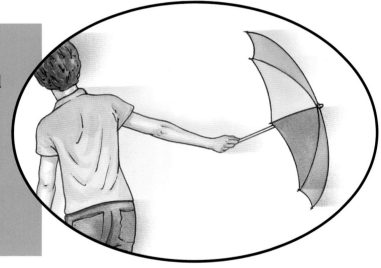

THE AMAZING FALLING NOTE
See how quickly streamlined shapes can move

Ask a friend to make a gap between their thumb and fingers. Hold a clean, new note just above the gap and say, "If you catch this you can have it."

The money falls so fast they miss it every time. Bend the note slightly at the bottom. This new non-streamlined shape slows down the falling note and your friend catches it easily.

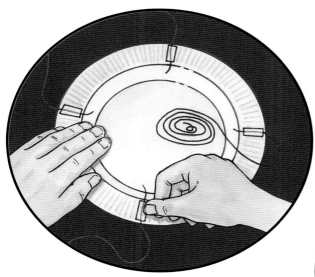

Figure 1

MAKE A PARACHUTE

Throw a light, unbreakable toy up and watch it fall straight down. Now tape four equal lengths of string to the edge of a paper plate (Figure 1). Attach the ends of the string to the toy (Figure 2). Stand on a chair and drop the parachute. Watch it drift down slowly (Figure 3).

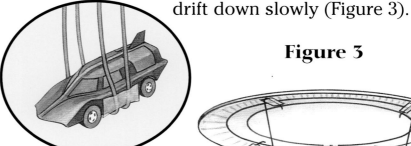

Figure 2

Figure 3

Air collects under the parachute, becomes squashed and pushes the parachute upwards. The compressed air pushes strongly enough to slow down the parachute's fall and soften the toy's landing.

Red hot!
Space shuttles re-entering Earth's atmosphere become red hot as air rubs against them. They have a heat resistant coat to prevent them from burning up.

Objects
travelling through the air can be shaped to speed them up (like a streamlined car) or to slow them down (like a parachute).

Air power

Moving air is a natural force that pushes against things and can make them move. Thousands of years before electricity was discovered, air power was used to push sailing boats along and to turn windmills. We still use it today. Burning coal, gas and oil for energy can pollute the atmosphere, and one day these fuels will be used up. Moving air is a source of power that is clean and will never run out. Huge wind farms use air power to produce electricity that we use in our houses.

Make a yacht with a sail to catch the wind

METHOD NOTES
Paint the plastic bottle with waterproof gloss paint and screw the cap on tightly.

Materials
- a plastic bottle
- scissors
- modelling clay
- a drinking straw
- coloured card
- a tall juice carton

1. Cut a rectangle out of the side of the plastic bottle for the body of the yacht (Figure 1).

2. Fix a piece of modelling clay on the bottom towards the lid of the bottle and push in a straw to make a mast (Figure 2).

Figure 1

Figure 2

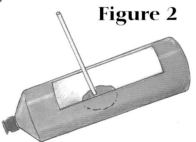

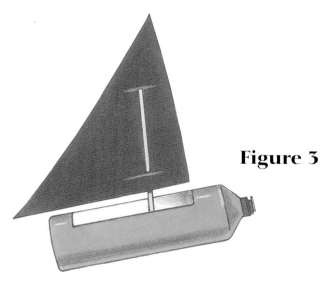

Figure 3

3. Cut a right-angled triangle for the sail. Make two holes in it and thread through the straw (Figure 3). Push the sail down slightly to curve it outwards.

4. Copy the wedge shape (Figure 4) onto the waterproof juice carton and cut it out to make a keel.

5. Fix the keel to the bottom of the boat with modelling clay. Attach a piece of clay to the other end (Figure 5).

6. Float the yacht in a bath. Blow into the sail and watch the yacht sail away from you.

Figure 4

Figure 5

WHY IT WORKS

A sail billows out as moving air pushes against it and powers the yacht through the water. Bigger sails catch more wind and make a yacht move faster.

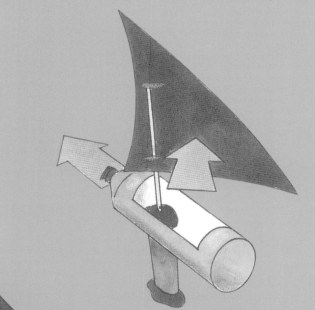

Sailors know how to move their sails to catch the wind, even when there is only a light breeze. Strong winds can be powerful enough to rip the sails. A keel helps to prevent the yacht from tipping over and keeps it moving forwards.

Air power

The power of moving air can be harnessed in many ways to make things work. Air blown downwards makes a cushion of air strong enough to lift a hovercraft.

MAKE A HOVERCRAFT

Make a hole in the centre of a square of card using a pencil (Figure 1). Glue a cotton reel over the hole (Figure 2). Cut out a circle of card, pierce a small hole in it and glue the card over the other end of the cotton reel (Figure 3). Blow up a balloon and wrap an elastic band around it to keep in the air. Stretch the balloon opening over the top of the cotton reel. Place the hovercraft on a table, remove the elastic band and release the air. The air escapes through the cotton reel and lifts the hovercraft off the table (Figure 4).

Figure 1

Figure 2

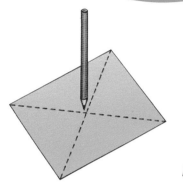

Figure 3

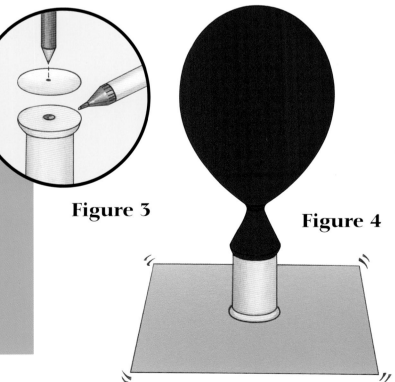

Figure 4

WHY IT WORKS

Escaping air from the balloon blows downwards through the cotton reel and creates a layer of air between the card and the table. The layer of air lifts up the hovercraft and it can move smoothly on its cushion of air. Try pushing it along while it is still hovering.

Air can turn on your television

Moving air turns the sails of a windmill to make electricity. These windmills are called turbines. One big, modern wind turbine can make enough electricity to supply a small town.

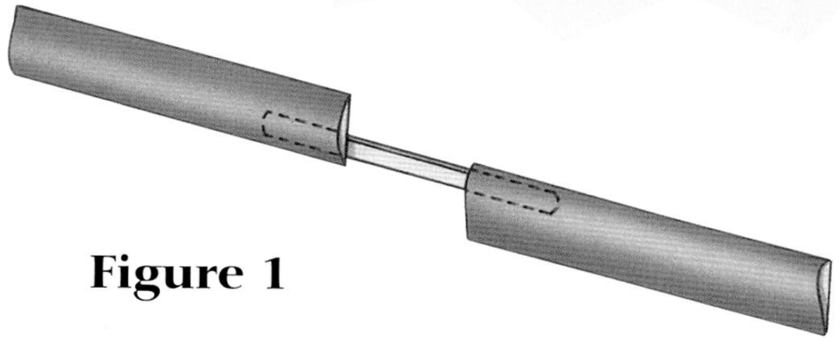

Figure 1

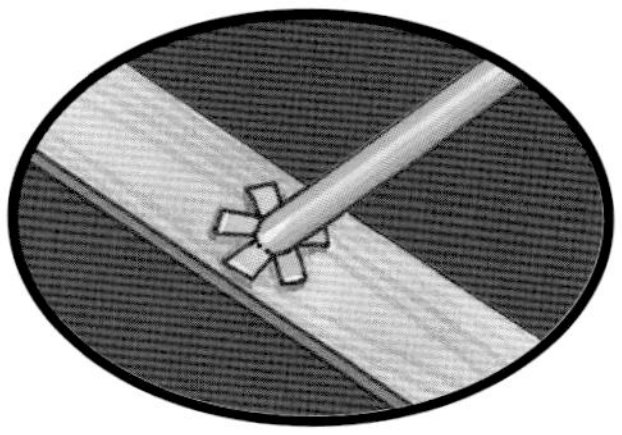

Figure 2

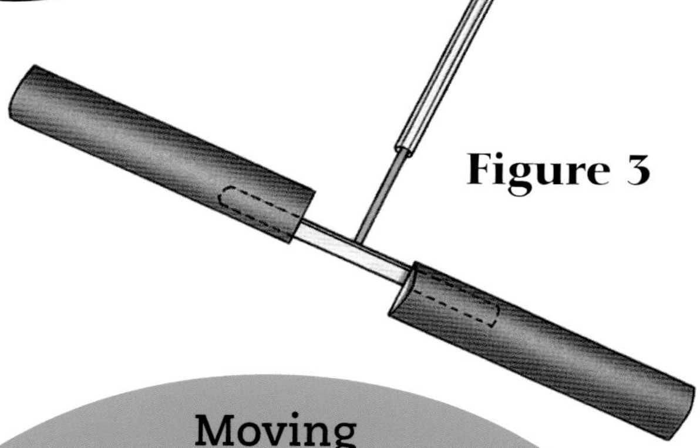

Figure 3

MAKE A WIND TURBINE

Attach two shaped wings (see page 34) to a lolly stick for the rotor (Figure 1). Glue a thin straw to the stick (Figure 2) and push it through a wider straw (Figure 3). Glue a cog to the other end (Figure 3). Hold the wide straw, take the turbine outside and watch it turn in the wind.

WHY IT WORKS

The wind turns your rotor and makes the cog turn. In the same way, the wind turns a wind turbine rotor which makes electricity.

Moving air can power a yacht, lift a hovercraft off the water and be harnessed to make electricity. Air also powers people, animals and plants. Without air there would be no life on Earth.

Glossary

Air pressure

A force caused by the weight of the atmosphere pressing down on the Earth.

Airtight

Not letting any air in or out of something. For example, sealing the lid of a bottle with some modelling clay makes it airtight.

Atmosphere

Layers of air about 700 kilometres deep that surround the planet Earth. It keeps us warm and protects us from the Sun's harmful rays.

Atom

The smallest complete particle of which everything is made.

Compressed air

Air becomes compressed when it is forced into a smaller space than it usually occupies. The air molecules move closer together.

Contraction

When particles that make up a substance move closer together and take up a smaller space. Air contracts when it cools.

Convection current

A circular movement of, for example, air. Warm air rises, cools and then falls again. This cycle is what causes the wind to blow.

Density

The weight, or heaviness, of an object per unit volume. A litre of water weighs more than a litre of air, so it is more dense.

Drag

Drag holds back moving objects. Vehicles that want to travel fast try to reduce drag.

Evaporation

When a liquid turns into a gas. This happens when liquids get warmer.

Expansion

When particles that make up a substance move further away from one another and take up a larger space. Air expands when it is heated.

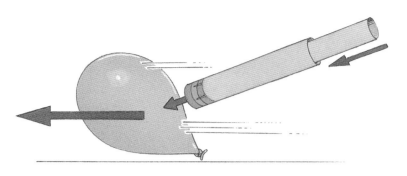

Friction

A force that occurs when two surfaces rub against each other.

Gravity

The pulling force of the Earth that makes things fall, and gives things weight. Gravity holds the atmosphere around the Earth.

Insulator

A material that keeps an object warm or cold. Insulators often have holes in to trap a layer of air. The trapped air stops heat being conducted in or out.

Molecule

A particle that contains two or more atoms joined together. Air contains molecules of many gases, including oxygen, carbon dioxide and nitrogen.

Streamlined

Describes an object that is shaped to reduce air resistance or drag and slip easily through air or water.

Thermal

A rising current of warm air. Gliders and some birds ride thermals to stay in the air.

Troposphere

The layer of atmosphere nearest the Earth. This is where weather takes place.

Vacuum

A completely empty space, with no gases, liquids or solids in it.

Index

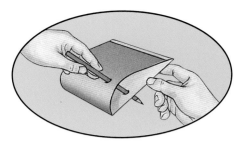